Volume 1

OBOE DUETS
Editor: James Brown

INDEX

CHESTER MUSIC

EDITOR'S NOTES

Nearly all the dynamic markings throughout are the suggestion of the editor. Where only one dynamic instruction appears, it applies to both voices.

Henri Brod. 1801 - 1839

Trained at the Conservatoire in Paris, his birthplace, he became an important figure in the development and improvement of the mechanism of the oboe.

Christian Ludwig Dietter. 1757 - 1822

Born in Ludwigsburg in Germany, Dietter originally studied painting before his interest in music was fully developed. He then became a violinist, also playing the bassoon. He wrote much music for wind instruments particularly for flute and bassoon. These duos are all based on music by Haydn.

Willem de Fesch. ? - c. 1758

A Flemish composer, he lived during the 18th century. In 1725 he was organist in Antwerp and later came to London where he lived for many years. He wrote several sets of Sonatas and Concerti for string instruments, including this movement originally for two flutes.

François Joseph Garnier. 1759 - 1825

He was born in France where he studied under Vogt at the Paris Conservatoire. He became principal oboe at the Opera, writing many pieces for the oboe. These are from his Tutor.

Laubach.

A composer of Victorian times who wrote many salon pieces for the piano, including this Polka, freely arranged by the editor.

Ignaz Joseph Pleyel. 1757 - 1831

Another prolific composer, he was the 24th child of an Austrian village schoolmaster. He learnt piano and violin under Vanhall in Vienna and became a pupil of Haydn. He travelled widely, and in 1792 visited London. Amongst his many compositions he wrote literally dozens of duets, including this one for flutes.

Georg Philipp Telemann. 1681 - 1767

A self-taught musician, he became one of the most prolific of all composers, writing more than 600 Overtures, 40 Operas, suites, and religious music.

Armand Vanderhagen. 1753 - 1822

Born in Antwerp, he lived much of his life in Paris where he worked as a clarinettist, writing and arranging many pieces for wind instruments. These pieces are all from his Tutor for the Oboe that was published in 1792.

1

ALLEGRETTO SCHERZOSO

Haydn-Dietter

JWC 55135

GIGUE IN G MAJOR

Telemann

3
RONDO

Pleyel

+ All grace notes to be played before the beat. However, they could at first be omitted.

ANDANTE FROM SONATA III

De Fesch

5
ANDANTE

TEMPO DI MENUETTO

Vanderhagen

ALLEGRETTO

Vanderhagen

8

RONDEAU IN C

Vanderhagen

9
RONDO FROM DUETTO V

Garnier

10
ALLEGRO MODERATO FROM DUETTO II

Garnier

GRAZIOSO E SOSTENUTO

Brod

12
ANDANTINO

13
ALLEGRETTO

Brod

14

CANON IN G

Oboe II begins to play when oboe I reaches bar 2(*)
and finishes at bar 99(⌢).

Telemann

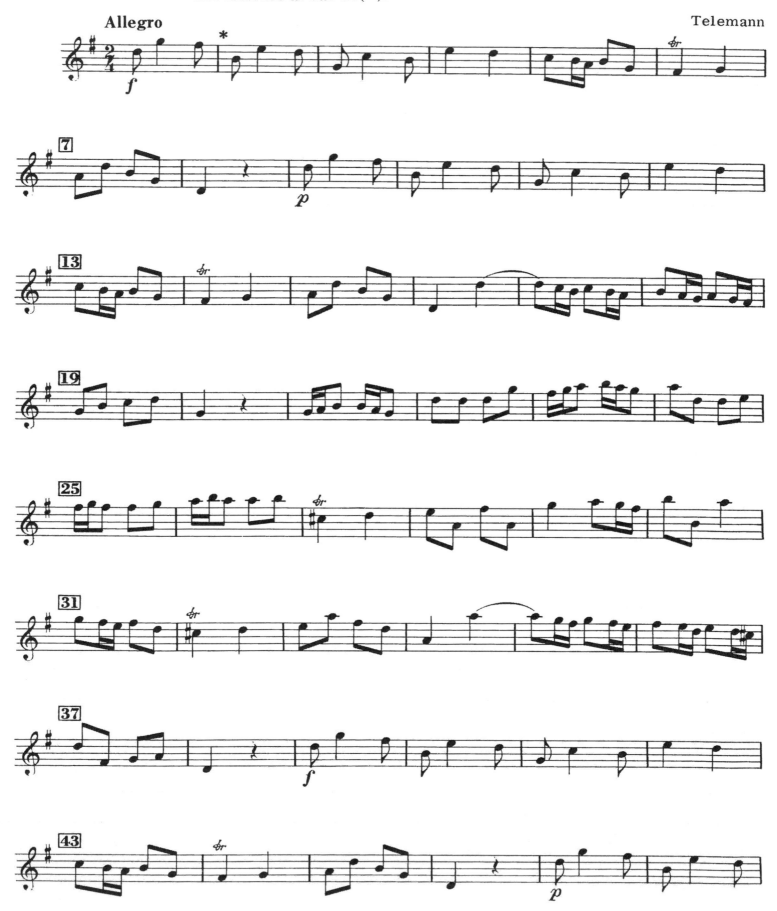

15
MENUET FROM SYMPHONY NO. 99

Haydn-Dietter

16
MODERATO CANTABILE FROM 'THE CREATION'

Haydn-Dietter

D.S. 𝄋 al Fine

17
POLKA-THE LITTLE GEM

Laubach-Brown